# Teen Code

## *A Rock Star's Life*

Lori A. Hoff

**Lori A. Hoff**
**1309 Main Street**
**Dallas, TX 75202**
http://www.nywusa.com

Publisher's Note: Names, characters, places, and incidents are a product of the author's imagination. Locales and public names are sometimes used for atmospheric purposes. Any resemblance to actual people, living or dead, or to businesses, companies, events, institutions, or locales is completely coincidental.

Ordering Information:
Quantity sales. Special discounts are available on quantity purchases by corporations, associations, and others. For details, contact the "Special Sales Department" at the address above.

**Teen Code/ Lori A. Hoff.** -- 1st ed.
ISBN 978-0-9962213-0-6

Library of Congress Control Number: 2015906224

*This book is dedicated to all young men
and women who are looking for wisdom
to make the right choices.*

**"Teach always; speak when necessary."**

**—Lori Hoff**

# CONTENTS

Intro

1: What About Your Friends? ..................... 1

2: Respect Yourself .................................. 7

3: Why You Mad? .................................... 13

4: What's Love Got to Do With It? ........... 17

5: The Keys to Honor.............................. 21

6: Work Hard, Play Hard......................... 25

7: The Right Choices .............................. 33

8: Don't Be a Bully ................................. 37

9: What About Sex?................................ 43

10: Who Has My Back? ........................... 47

The Rock Star's Teen Code

The Creative Team

About the Author

# Intro

Once upon a time not long ago there was an afterschool group of young people that decided to go on a walk. While on their journey they checked out a new trail and found a book that looked really old. As they read, they found out that it was a celebrity's guide to life. His name was Sol and he had a lot of money, a fleet of cars, personal trainers, chefs, and all the things that money could offer in life. He was the richest man who ever lived. If he was alive today he would have over a billion followers on all the social media networks. He had more money than Jay-Z, Beyoncé, the founder of Facebook, and Michael Jackson put together, so it is safe to say this guy was set for life. The good thing is, he took the time to write down the life skills and lessons he learned to keep him successful.

This immediately caught the attention of Karon, Anka, Jose, Angel, Franco, Lemar, Gabbie, Kristen, Freddy, and KB, the group of young people from OMI Worldwide's afterschool program. The book covered all kinds of topics and I invite you to read the students' discovery of answers to many of the questions they have about life.

# 1. What About Your Friends?

**KARON**
**grabbed the book and asked,**

What does the book say about friends? Some of mine are in question. I thought you had to do everything your friends wanted you to do but that is getting old quickly.

This book is saying something different, check out these helpful hints:

Never let loyalty and kindness leave you! Tie them around your wrist as a reminder. Write them deep within your heart. #Friends

Use common sense. If something doesn't feel right, it is probably for a reason. Trust your gut. #Friends

Be careful not to put your name on someone's debt. If your help depends on them paying you back, don't do it. #Friends

Watch out for constant liars. If they are lying to others, one day it will be your turn, and they will lie to you. #Friends

If you work hard and earn money, don't sign a loan for someone who is not working; it will ruin the friendship. #Friends

Doing good things for people wins friends. In order to have friends you must be friendly. Be the kind of friend you would want to have. #Friends

Stress weighs them down; an encouraging word cheers them up. #Friends

Laughter can uplift a heavy heart, but when the laughter ends, the grief remains. When your friend is down laughter can help them. #Friends

Through a tough time a good friend is still there. #Friends

Gentle words bring life and a shady tongue crushes the spirit of your friend. #Friends

A smile brings joy to the heart. Good news makes for good health. #Friends

Love grows when a fault is forgiven, but dwelling on it separates close friends. #Friends

There are 'friends' who destroy each other, but a real friend sticks closer than a brother. #Friends

A loyal friend is truly reliable but will you be that one? #Friends

An honest answer is like a kiss of friendship. A lie is like a smack in the face. #Friends

Don't pay someone back for what they've done to you or say, 'I'll get even with them.' You will only hurt yourself. #Friends

Just as damaging as a madman shooting a deadly weapon is someone who lies to a friend and then says, 'I was only joking.' #Friends

Wounds from a sincere friend are better than many kisses from an enemy. #Friends

It's better to live alone in the desert than with an arguing, complaining person. #Friends

# 2: Respect Yourself

**ANKA:**

Wow, that was cool. I think in order to be a good friend you also have to know yourself and who you want to be.

Check out this part on self-respect:

Take time to learn yourself and don't get caught up in doing what everyone else does. #Respect

The way of the fool is like total darkness. They have no idea what they are stumbling over. #Respect

Avoid all side talk. Look straight ahead and fix your eyes on what lies before you. Mark out a straight path for your feet; stay on the path. Don't get sidetracked, keep your feet from following the wrong thing. #Respect

Watch what you say or message, it displays who you ARE! #Respect

People who despise advice are asking for trouble; those who respect truth will succeed. #Respect

A person with good sense is respected; a treacherous person is headed for self-destruction. #Respect

Walk with the wise and become wise; associate with fools and find yourself in danger. #Respect

Discretion is a life- giving fountain to those who possess it, but discipline is wasted on fools. #Respect

The wise are cautious and avoid danger; fools plunge ahead with reckless confidence. #Respect

A glad heart makes a happy face; a broken heart crushes the spirit. #Respect

People who know themselves are patient and powerful and have self- control. #Respect

To acquire wisdom is to love oneself; people who cherish understanding will prosper. #Respect

Plans go wrong for lack of advice; many good mentors bring success. #Respect

Don't answer the arguments of fools, or you will become as foolish as they are. #Respect

A person without self-control is like a person jumping out of a plane with no parachute. #Respect

Young people who obey the law are wise; those with wild friends bring shame to themselves. #Respect

Choose a good reputation over great riches; being held in high esteem is better than money. #Respect

# B: Why You Mad?

**JOSE**

Self-respect is important, but what do you do when you are surrounded by angry people? One day I saw this guy minding his own business, chilling with his friends and some drama broke out and he got shot.

I was like, wow, this cat wasn't even doing anything! He was just at the wrong place at the wrong time. That scares me!

I need to check out this section on anger.

Short-tempered people do foolish things, and schemers are hated. #Anger

Spouting off before listening to the facts is both shameful and foolish. #Anger

Be careful with short-tempered people; they will do foolish things and regret them later. #Anger

People with understanding control their anger; a hot temper shows great foolishness. #Anger

A gentle answer shuts down anger, but harsh words make tempers flare. #Anger

A hot-tempered person starts fights; a cool-tempered person stops them. #Anger

Violent people mislead their friends, leading them to danger. #Anger

Angry people are eager for rebellion, but they will be severely punished. #Anger

Starting a quarrel is like the wind of a tornado so stop before a dispute breaks out. #Anger

Sensible people control their temper; they earn respect by overlooking wrongs. #Anger

Don't befriend angry people or associate with hot- tempered people, or you will learn to be like them and endanger your soul. #Anger

# 4: What's Love Got to Do With It?

**ANGEL**

What's love got to do with it? I want to know what the book says about love because the people who hurt me the most are the ones who claim to love me. Is that even possible? I'm so confused.

Do you see a section on Love?
Oh yeah, here it is...

Guard your heart, don't let just anybody in. Your heart will determine your life. #Love

Words can be deceiving but actions never lie. #Love

Love can be like a disease. If it is handled wrong it can sometimes cost you your life. #Love

There's truly a thin line between love and hate. Both take passion but have different results. #Love

Love the people who love you and remember, love gives and lust takes. Assess your situation and see if people are giving into your life or always taking. #Love

Love is patient, if someone is always pushing you to do something, run. #Love

Love believes the best in you and doesn't tear you down. #Love

Love is not forced. Love forgives; holding onto bitterness only hurts you. #Love

Love doesn't keep a record of wrongs, it lives in the present, not in the past. #Love

If someone loves you, they won't put their hands on you. #Love

Love takes time and patience to grow, it is not rushed. #Love

Love yourself first or no one else will be able to. #Love

# 5: The Keys to Honor

**Franco**

What's more important, love or honor? I want people to fear me but in a good way. I see all types of power and popularity contests but I think honor is the key.

Here is what the book says about honor:

The wise inherit honor but fools are put to shame. #Honor

"If a bird sees a trap being set, it knows to stay away." Be like a bird and fly out of there. #Honor

People with honor walk straight, others follow crooked paths and slip and fall. #Honor

Respecting people keeps you on earth long. #Honor

People who wink at wrong cause trouble, but a bold stance promotes peace. #Honor

People may be pure in their own eyes, but they must take time to examine their motives. #Honor

Loyalty makes a person attractive. It's better to be poor than dishonest. #Honor

Avoiding a fight is a mark of honor; only fools insist on quarreling. #Honor

Honor is no more associated with fools than snow with summer or rain with the desert. #Honor

The wise don't make a show of their knowledge, but fools broadcast their foolishness. #Honor

When there is corruption within a nation, its government falls easily, but wise and knowledgeable leaders bring stability. #Honor

Your actions determine how people treat you. Honor brings loyalty. #Honor

An honorable person gets mad respect. #Honor

# 6: Work Hard, Play Hard

**LEMAR**

Honor is cool Franco but I think it is all about the work… work hard, play hard, yuh know. I got to have my money right. I know the book has to talk about that. I want things man, nice car, big house, and the best clothes. I am trying to represent and I know money ain't falling out of the sky.

I am not trying to live on anybody's handouts. Feel me? I want some advice on that. I am trying to go hard. Is there a right way to do that?

Yeah, this is what I am talking about…

Get up and do something or when it comes time to eat you will be hungry. #Work

Stay hungry for work, just make sure it's legal and put your soul into all opportunities. #Work

Do your homework and know your dreams will be fulfilled. #Work

If you fold your hands and do nothing, poverty will overtake you. #Work

Ill gotten money has no lasting value. #Work

Lazy people are soon poor; hard workers get rich. #Work

Stolen water is refreshing and food eaten in secret tastes good but it is bitter in the end! #Work

The wise are glad to be instructed, but babbling fools fall flat on their faces. #Work

It is good for workers to be hungry; an empty stomach drives them on. #Work

Work smart and work during the summer so that during the school year you can focus on your education. #Work

Lazy people irritate their employers, like smoke in the eyes. #Work

Lazy people don't even look for work but the diligent make use of every opportunity they find. #Work

A hard worker has plenty of food, but a person who chases fantasies has nothing to eat. #Work

Wise words bring many benefits, and hard work brings rewards. #Work

Speaking with wisdom pays off and hard work brings a paycheck. #Work

Work hard and become a leader; be lazy and be broke. #Work

Taking away hope makes the heart sick, but a dream fulfilled is life to your soul. #Work

A smart person works at building a life for him or herself. A fool ruins his or her chances with bad words and actions. #Work

Work brings profit, but mere talk leads to poverty. #Work

A wise person is hungry for knowledge, while the fool feeds on trash. #Work

A lazy person's way is full of roadblocks, but a hard worker has an open highway. #Work

A little extra sleep, a little more slumber, a little folding of the hands to rest—then poverty will pounce on you like a bandit. #Work

Scarcity will attack you like an armed robber. #Work

As workers who tend an apple tree are allowed to eat the fruit, so workers who protect their employer's interests will be rewarded. #Work

If you love sleep, you will end in poverty. Keep your eyes open, and there will be plenty to eat! #Work

Intelligent people are always ready to learn. Their ears are open for knowledge. #Work

Enthusiasm without knowledge is no good; haste makes mistakes. #Work

Lazy people take food in their hand but don't even lift it to their mouth. #Work

Good planning and hard work lead to prosperity, but hasty shortcuts lead to poverty. #Work

# 7: The Right Choices

**GABBIE**

I feel ya. It's all about the green; that is the only thing that is going to get me out of my situation. I don't want my life limited, I am trying to reach for the stars and catch a few, stack my money so I can be set like our boy Sol here.

If I make good choices I should be set but sometimes I don't know what the right choices are.

Check out what the book says about money:

Give freely and become wealthier; be stingy and lose everything. #Money

If you can help someone who needs it, do it; don't be selfish. #Money

Lazy people want much but get little. Those who work hard will prosper. #Money

Thieves are jealous of each other's loot but good people are well rooted and bear their own fruit. #Money

It's senseless to pay tuition to educate a fool, since he has no heart for learning. #Money

It is better to have a little money, honesty, and love than to be rich and dishonest. #Money

Don't wear yourself out trying to get rich. Be wise enough to know when to quit. In the blink of an eye wealth disappears, for it will sprout wings and fly away like an eagle. #Money

The wealth of the rich is their fortress; the poverty of the poor is their destruction. #Money

The earnings of good people enhance their lives, but evil people squander their money on wasteful things. #Money

Saving adds up. If you saved $5 a week for about 77 years, you would have over $20,000.  #Money

Credit Cards are crazy. If you use credit to pay for $20 of fast food you could end up paying over $100 for that same meal. #Money

# 8: Don't Be a Bully

**KRISTEN**

Having money is cool but I am just trying to make it through high school. All this bullying and gossip can really make it hard. I am tired of friends who aren't loyal. I trust what they say and then get stabbed in the back. Just last week one of the guys from school didn't make it.

He committed suicide just to escape the bullying, which is something we face every day.

Hold up, I see a section on this; check it out y'all, this is deep...

Look for people whose words match their actions. #Bullying

Hiding hatred makes you a liar; slandering others makes you a fool. Too much talk leads to danger. Be sensible and keep your mouth shut. #Bullying

The lips of the good person speak helpful words, but the mouth of the ratchet speak perverse words. #Bullying

Smart people speak helpful words that are positive; gossip spreads negative trash. #Bullying

A gossiper goes around telling secrets, but those who are trustworthy can keep confidence. #Bullying

Don't make other people feel bad. It is not cool to bully your friends. #Bullying

Even a fool appears wise when they don't speak. #Bullying

Choose your words carefully; consider the outcome with what you simply have to say. #Bullying

An honest person doesn't lie intentionally but a gossiper breathes lies. #Bullying

An honest person saves lives but a gossiper is a traitor. #Bullying

Gossipers hate to be corrected, so they stay away from the wise. #Bullying

Honest people think carefully before speaking; the mouth of danger overflows with hurtful words. #Bullying

A troublemaker plants seeds of strife; gossip separates the best of friends. #Bullying

Don't envy evil people or desire their company. For their hearts plot violence, and their words always stir up trouble. #Bullying

Telling lies about others is as harmful as hitting them with a baseball bat, wounding them with a sword, or giving them a black eye. #Bullying

Interfering in someone else's argument is as foolish as yanking a dog's ears. #Bullying

A quarrelsome person starts fights as easily as hot embers light charcoal or as fire lights wood. #Bullying

A gossiper goes around telling secrets, so don't hang around with chatterers. #Bullying

Speak up for those who cannot speak for themselves; ensure justice for those being bullied. Yes, bullied. #Bullying

Watch your tongue and keep your mouth shut and you will stay out of trouble. #Bullying

# 9: What About Sex?

**FREDDY**

Yeah, that's deep but how about all these babies having babies and everyone thinking sex is the only thing to base our worth on? I am tired of all the pressure to constantly have sex and then deal with added drama from my partner. I know Sol has something to say about this because I need help.

One time I really wanted this girl and it was all I could think about. When my grades were slipping and I almost didn't pass to the next level she wasn't trying to hear it. I got depressed and couldn't get out so I am definitely interested in this topic.

Here goes…

Don't have sex with just anyone. You could wind up being so drawn physically and then fight every day because you can't stand each other. #Sex

You can get trapped by your own desires. Don't let them run you. You run you. #Sex

Sleeping with another person, man or woman can cost you your life. #Sex

The jails are full of people who made one wrong decision and never got back on track. #Sex

Don't be naïve. If someone is quick to give it up to you that comes from practice. #Sex

Don't get caught up; stay focused on your goals. The main thing that distracts people from their destiny is the wrong relationship. #Sex

Don't let your hearts stray away. Temptation has been the ruin of many; many men have been her victims. Her house is the road to the grave. Her bedroom is the den of death. #Sex

Don't be simple and follow everyone. Stand for something. #Sex

# 10: Who Has My Back?

KB

Yeah that's tough but you know what else is a struggle? Deciding if you should join a gang when you have no family who loves you and the gang members act like they are the only ones who care. Did they even have gangs back in Sol's day? Angel said her Uncle was killed in a gang and he gave his all for them.

I know she doesn't want me to go that route but it seems easy, like they will always have my back. At least that is what they told me.

I have to check this out....

Evil says, "Come and join us. Let's hide and kill someone! Just for fun, let's ambush the innocent! Let's swallow them alive, like the grave. Let's swallow them whole, like a pit of death. Think of the great things we'll get! We'll fill our houses with all the stuff we take. Come with us; we all get a share." #Gangs

The path of life leads upward for the wise; they leave the grave behind. #Gangs

Greed brings grief to the whole family, but those who hate bribes will live. #Gangs

Better to live humbly with the poor than to share stolen goods with the proud. #Gangs

The wicked take secret bribes to prevent the course of justice. #Gangs

Wealth created by a lying tongue is a vanishing mist and a deadly trap. #Gangs

The violence of the wicked sweeps them away, because they refuse to do what is right. #Gangs

Too much sleep clothes a person in rags. #Gangs

A prudent person foresees danger and takes precautions. #Gangs

The simpleton goes blindly on and suffers the consequences. #Gangs

A murderer's tormented conscience will drive him into the grave. Don't protect him! #Gangs

Stolen bread tastes sweet but it turns to rocks in the mouth. #Gangs

The trustworthy person will get a rich reward but a person who wants quick riches will get into trouble. #Gangs

The blameless will be rescued from harm, the crooked will be suddenly destroyed. #Gangs

The person who strays from common sense will end up in the company of the dead. #Gangs

# The Rock Star's Teen Code

The purpose of this book is to teach young people wisdom and life skills. When this book was written, wisdom used to be on the block, in the neighborhoods, and across the country. Nowadays who can find it? If you've got questions or need answers, this is the book for you. Wisdom will help you for a life-time and give you knowledge to make the right choices. You get strength by following common sense. If it doesn't feel right, it probably isn't. The words of the wise encourage many but fools are destroyed by their lack of knowledge.

***Doing wrong is fun for a fool, but living wisely brings pleasure to your soul.***

# The Creative Team

**Sophia**     **Lori**     **Kennedy**

Sophia Jose is a 20 year old graphic designer who lives in New York and digitized all of our characters. She attends Parsons – The New School for Design.

Kennedy is a 13 year old artist who drew our characters. She has been drawing since she was 4 years old and attends Danny Jones Middle School in Grand Prairie, Texas.

# About the Author

A native of Washington, NJ, Lori A. Hoff began her career with AT&T in 1995 and held a variety of positions in training, consumer services, and business sales. Hoff put herself through school and earned a Bachelor of Science degree in Ministry from Calvary Theological with and a Master's Degree in Child and Adolescent Therapy from Cornerstone University. During that time, she also founded a non-profit organization for at-risk youth, all while working full time.

Lori is currently a senior technical program manager within AT&T's technology group. She also serves as the National Mentoring Officer for the largest employee resource group, Women of AT&T.

Lori is also the CEO and founder of OMI and sits on the senior board for Big Brothers Big Sisters. She established a food pantry for the working poor in Middlesex County and also worked with the State of NJ as a therapist for at-risk youth, helping them to stay in school and become productive members of society. Lori has spent the last 15 years opening her home to youth and young adults who need a place to stay.

Additional copies of this book can be purchased from www.nywusa.com and online bookstores.

www.ingramcontent.com/pod-product-compliance
Lightning Source LLC
Chambersburg PA
CBHW072211090426
42740CB00012B/2485